Drive and Stro

Derbys....
The Peak District

*Other walking guides on the area
published by Countryside Books include:*

PUB WALKS IN DERBYSHIRE
Charles Wildgoose

PUB STROLLS IN DERBYSHIRE
Charles Wildgoose

ADVENTUROUS PUB WALKS IN THE PEAK DISTRICT
Charles Wildgoose

PEAK DISTRICT ILLUSTRATED WALKS
Trevor Yorke

PEAK DISTRICT TEASHOP WALKS
Charles Wildgoose

PUB WALKS FOR MOTORISTS: DERBYSHIRE,
NOTTINGHAMSHIRE & LINCOLNSHIRE
Charles Wildgoose and Roger Fox

Drive and Stroll in

Derbyshire &
The Peak District

·

Charles Wildgoose

COUNTRYSIDE BOOKS
NEWBURY BERKSHIRE

First published 2006
© Charles Wildgoose, 2006

COUNTRYSIDE BOOKS
3 Catherine Road
Newbury, Berkshire

To view our complete range of books,
please visit us at
www.countrysidebooks.co.uk

ISBN 1 85306 965 5
EAN 978 1 85306 965 9

Photographs by the author

Designed by Peter Davies, Nautilus Design
Produced through MRM Associates Ltd., Reading
Printed by Borcombe Printers Plc, Romsey

Contents

AREA MAP SHOWING LOCATIONS OF THE WALKS

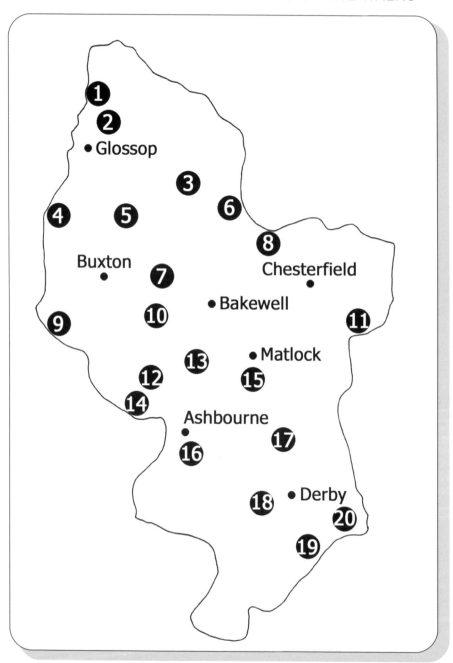

Contents ❧

Publisher's Note

We hope that you obtain considerable enjoyment from this book; great care has been taken in its preparation. Although at the time of publication all routes followed public rights of way or permitted paths, diversion orders can be made and permissions withdrawn.

We cannot, of course, be held responsible for such diversion orders and any inaccuracies in the text which result from these or any other changes to the routes nor any damage which might result from walkers trespassing on private property. We are anxious though that all details covering the walks are kept up to date and would therefore welcome information from readers which would be relevant to future editions.

The simple sketch maps that accompany the walks in this book are based on notes made by the author whilst checking out the routes on the ground. However, for the benefit of a proper map, we do recommend that you purchase the relevant Ordnance Survey sheet covering your walk. The Ordnance Survey maps are widely available, especially through booksellers and local newsagents.

Walking beside Dovestone Reservoir

This is my ninth walks book for Countryside Books and, once again, it has resulted in me visiting places I had never visited before and, hopefully you will be doing so too. There are some brilliant walks here and some awesome views.

So what is on offer? Well, there are three walks around reservoirs and then there are a few walks along trails and green lanes, namely the Parsley Hay and Minninglow circuits. You can walk on the start of the Pennine Way [Edale], the Round Dronfield Walk [Holmesfield], the Rowthorne Trail [Rowthorne], the Midshires Way [Black Rocks and Draycott] and the Trent and Mersey Canal [Weston on Trent].

The circuits range from 'very easy' to something a little more 'taxing'. Read the comments before tackling them and you should get an idea as to what to expect. I would always advise you to wear boots because some of the walks can get muddy – it's an occupational hazard, I'm afraid, in this part of the world.

And after your walk, why not relax and enjoy a good meal. Recommended places for refreshments are included with each route, and many start at a pub or teashop. Places to park are also detailed, some of which include a pub car park. Please remember, though, that if you do use a pub car park it is only polite to check with the landlord before leaving your car whilst you walk and, of course, you would be expected to return later as a customer.

Finally feel free to visit my 'Walking in Derbyshire' blog at **http://walking-in-derbyshire.blogspot.com/** – you will have the opportunity to post comments on it and see what's happening.

Enjoy these walks – I certainly did.

Charles Wildgoose

Acknowledgements

As ever I would like to thank my checkers. In particular I need to mention Graham and Ruth Rhodes, who have walked half of them (and their son Tom Rhodes, who was with them for much of the way). Thanks in particular to you three. There were others who have contributed though – Martin Pape, Geof and Stephanie Cole, Carole and Stuart Middleton, Mick Cooke and Gary Wigley (not forgetting their mate Graham), Ian Deuchar, Dave Williams, Kath Walker, Robert Walker, Julian Elliott and, probably the youngest checker, Jadey May Elliott. Thank you all very much.

Thanks must also go to Balkees for her support and for checking three or four of the walks too – and, as she pointed out, for walking most of the other routes with me!

Bridleway leading to the rocky chasm known as Lud's Church (see walk 9)

1 | Dovestone Reservoir

A view across Dovestone Reservoir

The Walk 2½ miles or 4¼ miles
Time: 2 hours for full route
Map OS Explorer OL1 Dark Peak GR 013036

How to get there

Dovestone Reservoir is reached from the A635 between Mossley and Holmfirth. Approaching from Mossley, drive north-eastwards and ½ mile beyond the Clarence in Greenfield fork right for the reservoir. **Parking:** In the car park at the reservoir.

Drive and Stroll

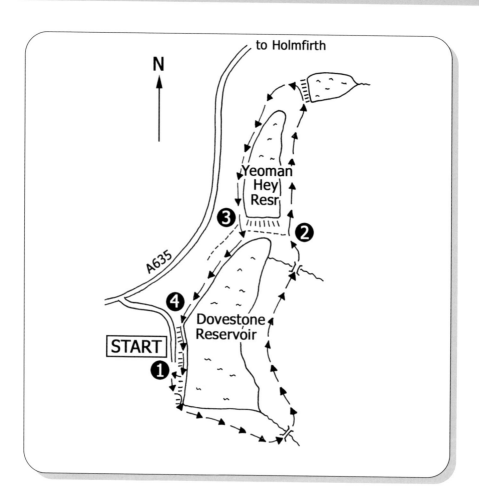

Introduction

Many of us will find it hard to believe that the Peak District is this far north – I certainly did. It's well worth making the trip though, as the scenery is spectacular. The walk circumnavigates Dovestone and Yeoman Hey Reservoirs (or just Dovestone if you want a shorter walk) on a track for part of the way and on fairly reasonable paths for the rest. You will pass a 'Life for a Life' Memorial Garden and later a Memorial Forest. On the full circuit you will get the chance to see a stone laid by the King of Tonga – a first for many of us, I should think. It's a fairly level walk so it shouldn't tax you too much.

Refreshments

The **Royal George** in Manchester Road, Greenfield is a J. W. Lees pub with a wide selection of food, such as Caribbean chicken or salmon salad. There are also vegetarian dishes, which include cheese and onion pie and vegetarian sizzler. From the reservoir car park, return to the A635, then turn left for 2 miles – the Royal George is on your left. Telephone: 01457 837851.

THE WALK

Walk to the top end of the car park and bear left up the steps to the dam wall. Then turn right to a tarmac access road 30 yards away, turning left along this. Pass the **Dove Stone Sailing Club building** on your left (you will often see 'Dove Stone' as an alternative form of 'Dovestone'). Ignore a farm entrance sharp right. Follow the public footpath along the track to the right of the boatyard. Pass the **Life for a Life Memorial Garden** on your left.

Life for a Life is a charity based in and around this area, providing memorial gardens and forests. The bereaved can remember a loved one by planting a tree or donating a bench. There is also the opportunity to arrange a planting to mark a special anniversary or similar event.

Then cross **Chew Brook** by a fairly substantial bridge. Turn left immediately along a tarmac path. Pass another **Life for a Life plantation**, a memorial forest, on your left. Stay on the stony path with the reservoir to your left. After ½ mile you reach **Ashway Gap**, where there used to be a house (Ashway Gap House). Cross the footbridge, continuing on the stony path. You reach a point where you can bear left across the dam wall between **Dovestone Reservoir** and **Yeoman Hey Reservoir**. *For the shorter walk,* turn left here and pick up the route at point 3.

If you're doing the whole circuit, then bear right on the footpath (without crossing the dam wall). Stay on this for ½ mile or so – it gets a bit stony here and there. **Yeoman Hey Reservoir** is to your left as you go.

Yeoman Hey was built in the 1880s, with Dovestone Reservoir following in the 1960s.

Beyond the end of **Yeoman Hay Reservoir**, fork left, ignoring a right fork uphill. The dam bank of **Greenfield Reservoir** should be above you. When you reach it, cross the bridge over a stream. Bear left on the track beyond. Where the track forks, take the right fork uphill. On reaching a gravel track turn left. Keep on this track until you come back to the banking between **Dovestone Reservoir** and **Yeoman Hey Reservoir** – after turning left, turn right almost immediately.

Drive and Stroll

Alderman's Hill in the far distance, from the path beside Dovestone Reservoir

Look out for the stone laid by the King of Tonga in 1981. It seems he was in this country to attend the wedding of Prince Charles and Lady Diana Spencer.

 ③

Stay in the direction you were heading. After 50 yards turn left through a kissing gate beside a farm gate – it's signed '**Dove Stone Car Park**'. This path leads you down towards the reservoir, with a plantation to your right. Continue for ½ mile to reach the overflow.

 ④

Turn sharp left at the end of the fence to cross the banking to return to the car park.

Places of Interest Nearby

You could head north-west to Uppermill to have a look at the **Huddersfield Narrow Canal**. There's plenty to see now that the canal has reopened to boats after having vast sums of money invested in it – money well spent in my opinion.

2 Longdendale

The overflow from Woodhead Reservoir and the footbridge you cross

The Walk 4¼ miles
Time 2 hours
Map OS Explorer OL1 Dark Peak GR 068983

How to get there

Take the B6105 north from Glossop. **Parking:** At the Peak Park car park at Torside Reservoir, on your right, 4 miles from Glossop.

Drive and Stroll

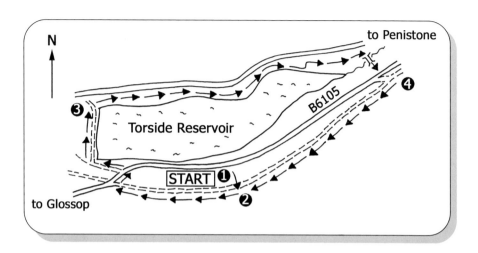

Introduction

This is a levelish route with no real difficulties – and plenty of fine views. You will be following the world famous Pennine Way for part of the walk – and it's not too testing, you'll be pleased to hear, at least not the bit you're going to be on. First off though you'll be walking on the Longdendale Trail. This is just over 6 miles long and forms part of the Trans Pennine Trail, which runs from the east coast (at Hornsea) to the west coast (at Southport). The reservoirs you will see today were all constructed in the mid to late 19th century to provide water for Manchester. A concessionary path which leaves the Pennine Way and passes through some lovely woodland, with the odd seat placed conveniently here and there, is quite delightful and gives marvellous views of Torside Reservoir.

Refreshments

The **Peels Arms** in Temple Street, Padfield. There's plenty of choice and the pub prides itself on serving locally produced home-cooked, freshly prepared food, such as steak, ale and mushroom pie and 'sausage trilogy'. They're open all day at weekends. Get there by following the B6105 back towards Glossop, and 2½ miles later take the first right for Padfield. Then take the second left to arrive at the pub car park on your left. Telephone: 01457 852719.

THE WALK

With the reservoir behind you, walk up to the top left-hand corner of the car park. Follow the path uphill towards the **Longdendale Trail**.

As already mentioned, this is part of the Trans Pennine Trail, which runs between Hornsea and Southport (just over 210 miles) with spurs to York, Leeds and Chesterfield. This Trail is also an extension to Euroroute 8, running from Holland to Northern Turkey – over 2,000 miles of walking. The Trans Pennine Trail West (or TPT, as it may be shown on some of the signs) runs from Southport to Barnsley. The Central and then the East sections take you through to Hornsea.

Walk through the **Life for a Life Memorial Forest** as you climb the slope towards the Trail.

The Life for a Life charity is based in and around this area (see Walk 1) – a nice way to remember someone.

Turn right on reaching the Trail and continue for ¾ mile. When you reach the B6105, walk alongside the road before crossing it and bearing right, with it now on your right. Follow the **Pennine Way** signs to turn sharp left down the tarmac access. (Don't turn left along the **Trans Pennine Trail West**!) Keep on the Pennine Way to cross the dam wall (with **Torside Reservoir** to your right and **Rhodeswood Reservoir** below to your left).

At the far side of the dam wall go up the steps on your right as the access road bends left. Cross a watercourse and continue to go up. The path splits. Ignore the one straight ahead beyond the turnstile; fork right along the **Pennine Way**.

The Pennine Way is the best known of all the long distance walking routes in this country. There's over 250 miles to be covered between Edale in the south and Kirk Yetholm in the north. It's probably one of the toughest walks too, and not to be undertaken by the inexperienced walker – but some of the countryside you will pass through is awe inspiring.

The path you're following swings right under the pine trees and is delightful, strewn with pine needles as it is. Leave the trees through a bridlegate. Walk 10 yards forward and pass through a kissing gate along the delightful '**Torside Concessionary Path**'. There is a road just above to your left. Descend some steps to cross a footbridge. Turn left alongside a channelled watercourse on your left. Continue for some distance to cross a concrete bridge over **Crowden Brook**. Walk towards a gate, bearing left on the path when you reach it. Some 40 yards before the road, turn right along

The concessionary path beside Torside Reservoir

The walks passes through some wonderfully remote countryside

the path for **Woodhead Dam**. Subsequently ignore a path to the left for **Crowden car park**. Some steps eventually lead you up to a footbridge crossing the overflow from **Woodhead Reservoir**. Rise up the concrete track beyond into the woodland. This leads you to the road.

 ④

Cross this and bear slightly left to reach the **Longdendale Trail** again. Turn right along this for **Torside car park** about a mile away. Take your pick as to which path you take back to the car – it's downhill to your right.

Places of Interest Nearby

Head back into **Glossop** and visit the **Heritage Centre**, where you can learn something about the town's history. Telephone: 01457 869176.

And how could I leave this area without mentioning **Hadfield**, just down the hill from Padfield. This is where the *League of Gentlemen* was filmed, with Hadfield passing for Royston Vasey!

3 | Ladybower Reservoir

Ladybower Reservoir

The Walk 5¾ miles
Time 3 hours
Map OS Explorer OL1 Dark Peak GR 173893

How to get there

Turn off the A57 Snake Road just west of the point where it is joined by the A6013 at Ladybower. Drive northwards beside the reservoir, signposted 'Derwent Valley'. **Parking:** This dead-end road reaches the Fairholmes car park after 2½ miles. This popular car park can be very busy at weekends and bank holidays – get there early!

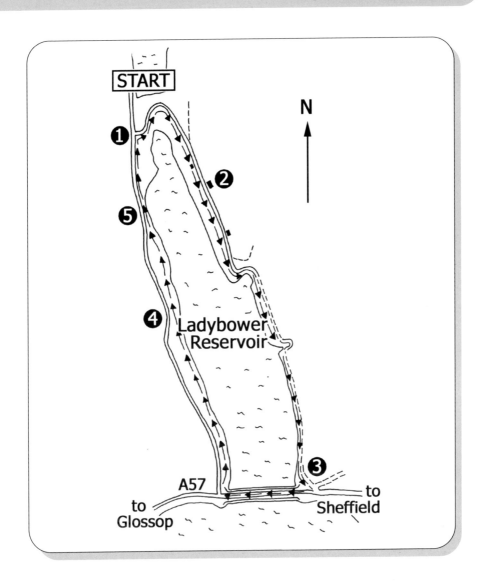

Introduction

This is a very level walk around Ladybower, with no climbs to speak of, giving you a chance to enjoy the delightful Peakland scenery from below. Although the route might seem a bit obvious, the things you will see on it will leave you well rewarded. Whilst it is the longest circuit in the book, it is easily undertaken and enjoyable throughout the year. Soon after you leave the car park go and have a look at the size of the stones in the dam wall of Derwent Reservoir, and buy one of the books describing how the dams were built when you get back to the Fairholmes Visitor Centre.

Refreshments

Visit the famous **Yorkshire Bridge Inn** at Bamford, to the south of Ladybower. To get there from the reservoir, return to the A57, turn left and then go right at the traffic lights onto the A6013. The inn is on your right after ¾ mile. It's a nice friendly place with good food, including specials such as chicken tandoori 'sizzler' and Italian chicken. Telephone: 01433 651361.

THE WALK

①

From the car walk to the **Visitor Centre**. Follow the path signed '**To Dams**'. On reaching the tarmac lane turn right. Head towards the wall of **Derwent Reservoir**.

With its two large stone towers this is quite an engineering feat. Either now, or on your return, go and have a closer look at the size of some of the stones in these towers. Derwent Reservoir was completed round about the time of the First World War. There are a number of pictorial books available for sale at the Visitor Centre.

Follow the road as it bears right and rises steadily. Ignore the sharp left turn – a bridleway leading to **Slippery Stones**.

 ②

Pass **Old House Farm** on your left. Then pass the old schoolhouse (now **St Henry's**). Ignore a footpath forking left, to stay on the lane as it descends

and bears left, then right around an 'inlet'. The tarmac track is now more of a stony one. Pass the path on your left signed '**Via Derwent Edge for Moscar'**. Stay on this track, still with the reservoir on your right. A mile or so later you reach a tarmac road beyond a gate; bear right down to the A57.

 ③

Turn sharp right over **Ashopton Viaduct**, and 400 yards later turn right again. Then, almost immediately, take the concessionary footpath for **Fairholmes**. Keep your dogs on the lead hereabouts. The views get better if anything on this side of the reservoir. Stay on the obvious path with the reservoir still on your right. Pass a valve house to your left – water can be diverted into another pipe here if repairs are necessary. Your path then forks right off the grassy track you've been following. As you go, the path literally runs between the 5 ft high pipes of the **Derwent Valley aqueduct**.

The aqueduct carries water down to the East Midlands. As you will see,

Across Ladybower Reservoir

the pipes were made at Staveley in Derbyshire, and feel free to give them a knock – they're pretty solid.

④

You then walk very near the road on your left, but the path soon bears

away from it. Eventually, ½ mile later, the path brings you back to the road, by a car park.

⑤

Turn right here to get back to the **Fairholmes car park**.

Places of Interest Nearby

You could explore the **Derwent** and **Howden** dams further up the valley. These were made famous of course by the dambusters who used them for practice runs during the Second World War. You may also see the memorial to 'Tip', a sheepdog who stayed with the body of his owner, in the snow, for 15 weeks between December and March in the early 1950s – we don't get winters like that nowadays. Though we don't want to wear you out, why not go for a bike ride after the walk? Call the Visitor Centre (in the Fairholmes car park) on 01433 651261 or email cyclehire@peakdistrict.gov.uk

4 Lyme Park

Looking back to Knightslow Wood from Park Moor

The Walk 3¼ miles
Time 2 hours
Map OS Explorer OL1 Dark Peak GR 963824

How to get there

Lyme Park is just off the A6 between Disley and High Lane. Look out for the signs and then follow the 1½ mile drive southwards to the large car park with the Hall to your left. **Parking:** There's a fee payable unless you are a National Trust member.

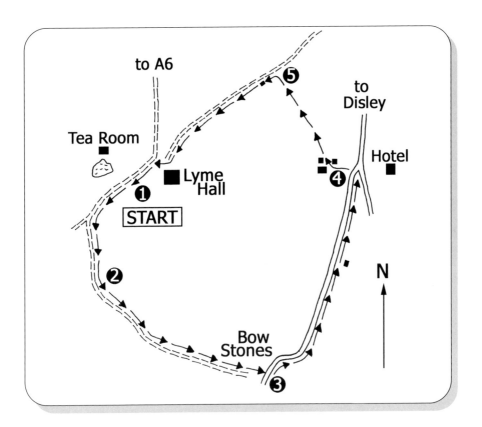

Introduction

This is a very popular area on the edge of Stockport. After a steady ascent into Knightslow Wood, you then continue to climb as you go up onto Park Moor. Take your time, though, and look behind you to see the planes flying into and out of Manchester Airport. After this the walk gets easier and you will soon be looking at the twin stumps of the Bow Stones, a couple of ancient crosses that could probably tell us a story or two. A steady descent on a quiet lane brings you to a drive, along which you follow the well waymarked 'Alternative route' for the Gritstone Trail. After that you enter Lyme Park again, at East Lodge, and have a lovely walk back to Lyme Hall along a gravel track. On the way you get a good view of The Cage, a tower that was built in the mid 18th century and a good place (then) to watch the deer hunt.

Drive and Stroll

Refreshments

Visit the National Trust **Workshop Yard Coffee Shop** at Lyme Park. Light meals are available here and you can eat either indoors or out. There are jacket potatoes with various fillings, bacon butties, or salads, which are probably better for the figure. Throw all the good work away by trying some banana or apple cake – both delicious. Telephone: 01663 762023 (ask for the coffee shop).

THE WALK

From your car follow the tarmac road between the car park and the pond in a southerly direction. Immediately before a cattle grid turn left uphill to pass through a kissing gate by a larger gate. This is signed '**Gritstone Trail**'. Proceed up the stony track, ignoring a grassy track to the right. As you rise, with a plantation on your left, you should have a good view over your right shoulder.

The Gritstone Trail, which incorporates the former Mow Cop Trail, is a splendid 35 mile ridge walk between Disley and Kidsgrove.

Follow the track into **Knightslow Wood** and proceed through the trees. Ignore a path sharp left as you go, but enjoy the view along it. Leave the wood by a ladder-stile. Follow the track (signed for **Bowstones**) out of the wood. Stay on it as it rises for ½ mile across **Park Moor**. Although it is a steady climb you will be rewarded with some marvellous views behind you as you proceed. Leave the moor by a ladder-stile beside a gate. Walk to the lane ahead.

Turn left along this and after a few yards look out for the **Bow Stones** on your left.

These are described as two shafts of late Saxon crosses, that were probably landmarks or boundary stones as well as objects of devotion. The heads of the crosses in the courtyard of Lyme Hall are likely to be from the Bow Stones apparently.

You are now looking at a different view – **Whaley Bridge** being the town to your right in the valley. Proceed on the lane for ¾ mile until you reach the entrance to **Moorside Grange** – a rather incongruous sight hereabouts.

Turn left up the farm driveway signed '**East Lodge**'. It's an alternative route for the **Gritstone Trail**, so you should be able to follow the waymarks for this part of the walk. (Just in case they are missing, follow these instructions!) Walk into the farmyard and turn right to pass through a gate. This brings you into a field. Aim for the stone outbuilding ahead with the 'bull's-eye' window. Don't leave the field you're in though; pass some 50 yards to the

Lyme Park

right of the building. Keep on down through the rushes to cross a stile on your left into a small beech wood. Walk forward for 20 yards (there are the remains of buildings here). Turn right after crossing a stream to reach a metal kissing gate. In the field beyond, keep straight ahead, bearing *very* slightly away from the fence on your right. Stay on the same level through the field you're in, bearing gently round to your left to cross a dry ditch beneath some trees. Turn left immediately to enter another field, turning right straight away to walk alongside a broken line of trees on your right. Head towards a single wooden electricity pole ahead, passing through a gap in the wall. Keep to the right of the pole to reach a stile, which you negotiate to reach a walled track beyond.

Turn left on the track to re-enter **Lyme Park** at **East Lodge**. Stay on this main track all the way back to **Lyme Hall**. As you go, to your right is **The Cage**. On reaching the Hall follow the road down to the car park.

Places of Interest Nearby

Lyme Hall (National Trust) itself is well worth visiting, as are its gardens. For details of opening times, telephone: 01663 762023.

5 Edale

One of the outstanding views on the route

The Walk 3¾ miles
Time 2 hours
Map OS Explorer OL1 Dark Peak GR 124853

How to get there

Follow the Edale road north from the A6187 at Hope. Stay on this for 5 miles to reach Edale's village centre. **Parking:** There is a pay and display car park on the right as you enter Edale.

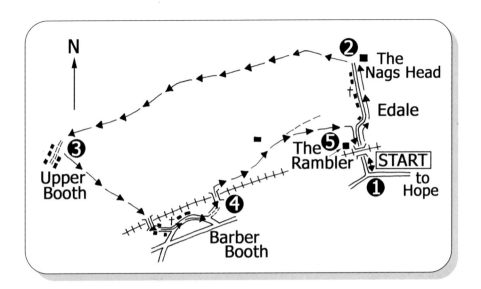

Introduction

A section of the Pennine Way forms part of this route but it isn't too strenuous – just take it steady and pace yourself. The walk heads up through the village to the Old Nags Head, which is the start of the Pennine Way. Just another 250 miles to go to get to the other end! You then set off across a field, rising slowly, whilst all around you there are marvellous views of the surrounding countryside – look there's Mam Tor and over there, Lose Hill . . . there's stupendous Peak District scenery in every direction. Then you descend into Upper Booth where you may want to wander around for a few minutes off the route before heading gently across the fields to reach Barber Booth (a 'booth' round here refers to a (very) small village). You cross and recross the railway line (using footbridges) before following a flat path back to Edale itself. As you go though, all around there is great scenery, and you can take your time and just marvel at the countryside you will be enjoying. You can always save a walk up on to Kinder Scout till the next time you come up this way.

Drive and Stroll

Refreshments

The **Rambler Country House Hotel** in Edale is very popular with visitors and welcoming to walkers, inside and out. If the sun's shining sit outside and enjoy the scenery, watching people come and go. The bar menu provides a lot of choice. There are some great dishes on offer, among them a trio of pork sausages, 100% beef burgers and home-made rambler pie with peas and chunky chips. Telephone: 01433 670268.

THE WALK

From the car park head out onto the road past the toilet block. Turn up the road past the **Rambler Country House Hotel** on your left. Then pass **Fieldhead campsite** and the new **Visitor Centre** on your right. Keep on up the lane. Pass between the church and the old churchyard.

On reaching the **Old Nags Head** you've got to the start of the **Pennine Way**.

The Pennine Way crosses some of the most isolated areas in England and shouldn't be attempted except by the fittest of walkers who can use a map and compass and who know how not to get lost!

Turn left a few yards before the pub on the path signed for '**Upper Booth and Pennine Way**'. Pass through a kissing gate almost immediately and walk uphill beside a small brook. After going through a wicket gate turn left, following the Pennine Way 'acorn' waymarks. **Broadlee Bank Tor** rises above you, and the **Edale valley** is to

your left. Follow the obvious path through the fields for the next ¼ mile to reach a more open grassy area with a steep bank to your right. Keep straight forward along the **Pennine Way** (and **Jacob's Ladder**) path, ignoring a right fork for **Crowden Brook**. Cross a step-over stile as a wide valley opens out before you. Follow the obvious path down. After crossing another step-over the path begins to descend more directly towards the valley. Eventually the Pennine Way follows a track down towards **Upper Booth**, a small collection of properties. On reaching a stony track, turn left down it for 15 yards.

Pass through a wicket gate beside the farmgate on your left. In the first field head just to the left of **Mam Nick** (the 'nick' in the horizon ahead).

As you walk towards Mam Nick you may be able to make out the remains of the ancient hillfort on Mam Tor. What a marvellous place it must have been to keep an eye on the surrounding countryside.

In the second field head almost directly towards the Nick. Walk along the right side of fields three and four, before bearing slightly right in the fifth field to pass through a wicket gate. In the sixth field follow a grassy track, still aiming towards the Nick. Stay on this track now until it takes you alongside the railway, then over it at **bridge 59**. Stay on the track, walking directly through the farmyard (of **Whitmore Lea Farm**). Keep forward along a tarmac lane, ignoring a track forking right. Pass **Edale Methodist chapel** on your left to come out onto a narrow lane in **Barber Booth**.

Turn left. Immediately beyond **Brookfield**, bear left up a track for **Grindsbrook Booth** and **Edale Station**. Cross **bridge 58**. Pass through a kissing gate on your right just beyond

and follow the path along the left side of the narrow field. Keep on the bottom side of the second field, continuing across the third field and along the bottom side of the fourth. In the next field (with a farm at the top), bear slightly left to the stile opposite. Cross the bridge and farm track beyond and head for the stile 30 yards away. In the field beyond walk alongside the fence on your right for 10 yards – keep along this line (ignoring a stile which is a quarter left of you) to cross the right hand of the two stiles. Then walk along the left side of the fields ahead to reach the road.

Turn right down the road back to the **Rambler** and the car park.

Places of Interest Nearby

Drive over to **Castleton**, on the other side of Mam Tor, and visit some of the caverns there. You could start off by visiting the **Devil's Arse** and ask one of the guides why it's called this (it used to be known as Peak Cavern). Telephone: 01433 620285. Then there are the remains of 11th-century **Peveril Castle**. Telephone: 01433 620613.

6 Redmires Reservoirs

Beside the conduit at Redmires

The Walk 2 miles
Time 1 hour
Map OS Explorer OL1 Dark Peak GR 256856

How to get there

Follow Ringinglow Road westward from the A625 in Sheffield. At Ringinglow take the right turn. After that keep left at each road junction to reach the Redmires Reservoirs. **Parking:** The car park you are heading for is beside the most westerly of the three reservoirs. It's on the right just before a left-hand bend – don't park at the first car park you reach on your right.

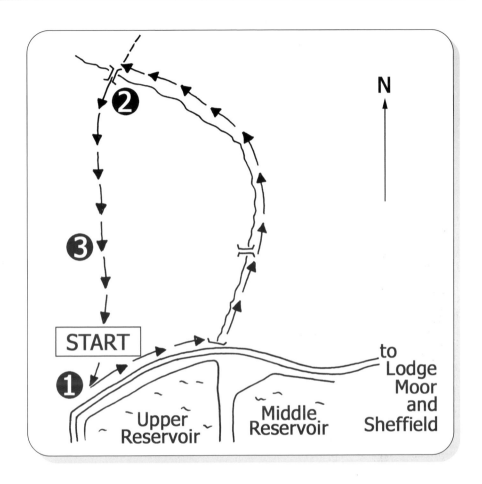

Introduction

This is one of the shortest strolls in the book and very enjoyable – a steady amble through delightful countryside. Starting off alongside the westernmost Redmires reservoir, you'll soon be walking at the side of a conduit as you get out onto the moorland. Just when you're wondering if you're going to keep going all the way into the Peak Disrict, you suddenly do a left turn onto the moor and before you know it – you're back. There's not much more to say – don't lose any time in setting out and exploring this lovely area on the edge of Sheffield.

Drive and Stroll

Refreshments

Visit the **Three Merry Lads** at Lodge Moor. It's a nice pub, friendly, with some tasty food – snacks, light bites and light dishes. Try the tortilla wraps or the Creole prawns. There are also sandwiches and jacket potatoes. To get there, turn left out of the car park and keep on the road (Redmires Road), ignoring a road to the right, until you reach the pub on your left. Telephone: 0114 2302824.

THE WALK

Turn left from the car park along the track with the reservoir on your right.

This is Redmires Upper Reservoir, which was completed in the mid 19th century. It holds over 300 million gallons of water.

After 400 yards, at the end of the reservoir, turn left along the footpath running beside the conduit on your left. This is an easy access track that takes you for nearly a mile to a crossing path. As you go, to the right there are good views across to the western outskirts of **Sheffield**.

On reaching a bridge (and with a footpath to your right onto the

Walking beside the conduit at Redmires

moorland and open access land in front of you), turn left over the bridge and follow the grassy track rising gently through the heather. This runs alongside a wall on your right, though after 200 yards it bears slightly left away from it. Now you should be aiming for a wall some 200 yards ahead. On reaching this wall walk up the banking in front of you, with the wall to your left. At the top of the banking the path levels out. Continue beside the wall until you reach a boggy area in a valley.

Cross this via the duck-boarding and rise up the valley side ahead – keeping the wall on your left. Continue beside this until you get back to the car park. As you go you will get a good view of all three reservoirs in the valley, half left of you.

Places of Interest Nearby

The **Botanical Gardens** in Sheffield offer 'stunning collections of trees and shrubs set in a historic landscape created in 1836'. They are near to the Royal Hallamshire Hospital, a mile south-west of the city centre. Telephone: 0114 2676496.

7 | Miller's Dale

Descending the path into Miller's Dale

The Walk 4¾ miles
Time 2½ hours
Map OS Explorer OL24 White Peak GR 139733

How to get there

Follow the A6 westwards from the Taddington bypass. Pass the Waterloo pub on your left. After ½ mile turn right on the B6049 and continue down into the valley. **Parking:** After crossing the River Wye, turn left uphill to Miller's Dale car park.

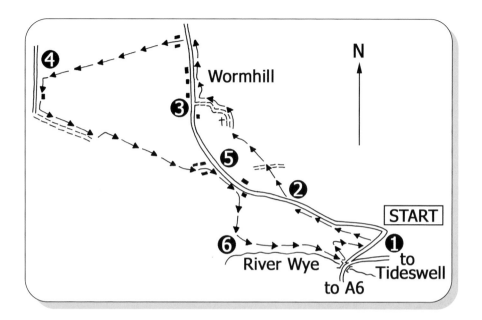

Introduction

This route is in prime Peak District countryside, with plenty of interest in a beautiful part of the world. After leaving the car park, a path and then a fairly quiet lane bring you to a footpath leading across the fields to the lovely village of Wormhill. Here there's a memorial to James Brindley, the creator of some marvellous canals. Follow the Pennine Bridleway out of Wormhill before circling round and coming back into the village. After this you descend into Miller's Dale itself. You then stroll beside the River Wye for ¾ mile or so until you climb some steps back to the car park, having completed an excellent walk.

Refreshments

Try the **George Hotel** in Commercial Road, Tideswell, to the north of Miller's Dale. To get there, drop down the hill from the car park and turn left at the junction. Follow the road all the way into Tideswell – the George is on your left, next to the church. It's a popular destination for locals and villagers alike. They sell Hardy & Hanson beer and offer a range of food from bowls of home-made soup to more substantial fare like steak and Kimberley ale pie, lasagne, haddock and a roast of the day. Telephone: 01298 871382.

Drive and Stroll

THE WALK

①

Walk to the car park entrance and turn sharp left on the path, climbing the steps. Follow the walled path ahead for 300 yards. Then bear half right up to the road. Turn left along the lane for ⅓ mile.

②

Immediately beyond a farmgate on your right pass through the squeezer stile. Walk along the right side of the small field, bearing half left in the second field. Keep in the same direction across the corner of the third field. Keep in the same direction across the fourth field to reach a walled track. Turn left for 5 yards, then right through another squeezer. Stay in the same direction in the fifth field to reach a step-over in the far corner. With your back to the stile in the sixth field, walk to the far left corner. Here there's a gate. Follow the track beyond as it bends round to the left to reach the entrance to St Margaret's church.

Do walk round the churchyard, as there are some interesting old gravestones here, one of which is inscribed 'James Roger Ball died at Wormhill Hall Oct 20th 1862 Aged 59. In memory of a faithful valued servant'.

Continue to the road.

③

At the road in **Wormhill**, turn right along a path below the road.

There is a memorial here to James Brindley (1716–1772). He was born at Tunstead nearby and became one of the foremost engineers of English canals. He came from a Quaker background, his great grandmother being a Bowman from Leek.

Pass the old stocks and head up the main street for 300 yards. Turn left up the driveway to **Old Hall Farm**, following the **Pennine Bridleway**.

This is the first national trail created specifically for horses, mountain bikes and boots. It will eventually run from the High Peak Trail to Northumberland – a distance of some 350 miles.

At the top of the farmyard bear half left through a gate. Follow the stony track leading uphill to pass through further gateways into a field. Walk beside a wall on your right. Enter a second field and continue forward.

Ahead are Old Moor and Tunstead quarries. Whilst to some extent they are a blot on the landscape, at the same time it has to be said that there is something rather impressive about their scale. Tunstead is probably one of the largest quarries in this country, perhaps Europe.

The Brindley Memorial in Wormhill

Pass through the right hand of two gates facing you, walking beside the wall on your left beyond. Continue along the walled track at the end of the third field to reach a lane.

 ④

Turn left here (after noting the water trough directly ahead). After 300 yards bear left along the tarmac bridleway, with trees on your right. Continue for 400 yards and, as the bridleway bears right, uphill, keep straight forward along the grassy verge to reach and enter the end of the narrow field on your left. Walk down to the bottom corner and turn right over a stile. With your back to the stile, aim slightly left towards a gap in the wall (just to the left of the valley bottom).

Pass through this and, keeping in the same direction, pass through a squeezer between a trough and a gate. Follow the track beyond to reach **Hassop Farm**. Keep straight ahead here, bearing half left at the end of some buildings and passing the farmhouse on your left. Then bear right across the lawn to reach a wicket gate. You are now back in **Wormhill**.

 ⑤

Turn right down the road for 75 yards to turn right again down the footpath for **Cheedale** and **Blackwell**. This brings you to the **Derbyshire Wildlife Trust reserve**.

The Derbyshire Wildlife Trust looks after nearly 40 nature reserves in the

*county and has over 10,000
members. The Trust organises
regular working parties of volunteers,
and I myself have worked with
friends from the Derbyshire Dales
Group of the Ramblers' Association
to help the Trust clear hawthorn
from this very hillside. Log on to
www.derbyshirewildlifetrust.org.uk
for further details.*

Descend until you come out from
under the trees. Ignore a path turning
sharp right here. Continue forward
along the level path into the open.
Then descend a (sometimes slippery)

path to the **River Wye** in the valley
bottom.

Turn left along the riverside path. The
river should be on your right for a
good ½ mile. As you go, ignore some
steps on your left leading back to
Miller's Dale Station. Pass under the
bridge and proceed until you reach a
road. Immediately before the road
turn left up the steps back towards
the car park. At the top of the steps
bear right to reach the station building
and the car park beyond.

Places of Interest Nearby

It would be well worth looking round **Tideswell church** which is known as
the 'Cathedral of the Peak'. It is one of the largest in the area and was all
but completed by the end of the 14th century. It contains some
interesting carvings and memorials. It's right next to the pub, so you
can't miss it.

8 | Holmesfield

There is a lovely atmosphere through Holmesfield Park Wood

The Walk 3¾ miles
Time 2 hours
Map OS Explorer OL24 White Peak GR 320777

How to get there

Holmesfield is just south of Sheffield. Take the B6054 eastwards from Owler Bar on the A621. **Parking:** In the pub car park behind the Angel Inn or on the roadside nearby.

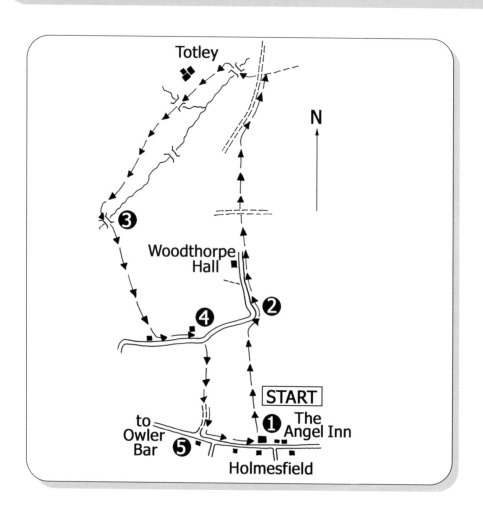

Introduction

This is a fascinating walk through a not very well known area on the edge of the Peak District, which is just 1½ miles away. The route starts off along an easy access trail, which descends through Holmesfield Park Wood. Whether you walk this in sunshine or mist, it's lovely woodland, full of atmosphere, particularly when it's misty. Later you join an old pitched way, which is probably an ancient route. Just as you think you're going to walk into Totley, the walk swings southward and you find yourself in another attractive wood. After this the route opens out and you're heading back across the fields for

Holmesfield. As there's quite a bit of woodland walking, take your boots for sure on this walk unless there's been a dry spell.

Refreshments

The **Angel Inn** in Holmesfield is a friendly place, and can get very busy at the weekend. The food is excellent and includes some more unusual dishes such as Kashmiri lamb shank and braised vegetables with cider dumplings. It is closed on Mondays. Telephone: 0114 2890336.

THE WALK

①

From the pub car park turn right between the concrete gateposts along the track.

This is part of the Dronfield 2000 Rotary Walk, and this section is also an easy access trail. All told, the whole of the Dronfield Walk is 14½ miles in length. It's an excellent initiative. This first section is available for the less able to undertake a short linear walk, with a pick-up point just over ½ mile away from the car park in Holmesfield.

Where the track forks keep left, passing through a kissing gate to the right of the property known as **Holmesfield**. Enter ancient **Holmesfield Park Wood**. Stay on the gravel path descending for nearly ½ mile through the wood.

②

On reaching a lane, bear right along it. Ignore a footpath to the left. Stay on the lane, passing **Woodthorpe Hall** to your left. Continue straight forward along the public footpath, passing a

farmyard on your right. Stay on the path, a sunken lane under a canopy of leaves. Cross a farm track and continue until you're descending on an old pitched surface. On reaching a track turn right. After 400 yards you reach a step-over stile on your right; turn left here into the trees. Bear right, crossing a footbridge over **Totley Brook**. This brings you to the back of some houses; before you reach them turn left along the gravel path. You should then walk between brook and houses. Stay on the main path. Cross a wooden footbridge over a small stream running into the brook to enter a wood. Follow the wide(ish) path beyond, and 300 yards later ignore a wooden footbridge to your left. Some 500 yards after this bridge (with a patchy strip of concrete 10 to 12 yards long running along the left side of the path), turn left under a stand of conifers. (If you reach a path coming in from the right 50 yards beyond these conifers you've gone too far!) Cross the brook by a footbridge and enter the field beyond.

③

Walk up the right side of the field ahead, then a second and a third.

Drive and Stroll

Chatsworth House is well worth a visit after your stroll

Enter a lawned area with a long stone outbuilding ahead. Keep to the left of this, passing onto the gravel drive beyond. Bear left to the lane and turn left along it.

 ④

Just beyond a property on the left, on a left-hand bend, turn right, climb a stile and walk up the field with the wood immediately to your left. Keep up the left side of a second and then a third field. As you go, you may catch a glimpse of the sunken bridle road just inside the wood. At the top of the third field join the bridle road and keep forward up to the road.

 ⑤

Turn left back to the **Angel**.

Places of Interest Nearby

Head approximately 6 miles south and visit **Chatsworth House** (or the park if the house is closed). It is reached via the B6012, which runs south from the A619 west of Chesterfield. There's plenty to see – the house, the garden, a farmyard, an adventure playground, all open from mid March to November. Telephone: 01246 565300.

9 | Wincle

A view of the lovely countryside near Danebridge

The Walk 4½ miles
Time 2 hours
Map OS Explorer OL24 White Peak GR 962653

How to get there

Wincle is reached off the A54 between Buxton and Congleton. Approaching from the north-east, turn off left at the crossroads, signed for Wincle. At the church turn left, signposted to Danebridge. **Parking:** On the roadside just below the Ship Inn.

Drive and Stroll

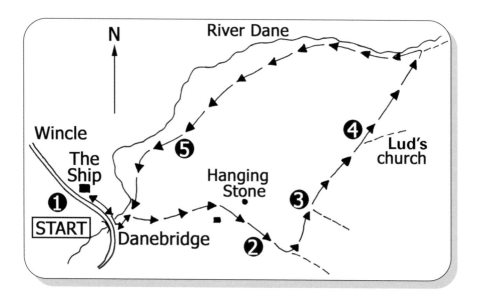

Introduction

This is a lovely, lovely area. If you've not been before you'll wonder why. It's a bit rockier than some of the other walks but you will be rewarded with fine views and fascinating sights. Initially you climb away from the River Dane before crossing some open moorland with splendid vistas across the valley. A decision looms: do you visit Lud's Church or not? Go on – if you've not been you'll enjoy it. Lud's Church is a chasm, though whether it was ever used for religious purposes by Lollards or anyone else is lost in the mists of time. It would certainly have been a well known landmark and presumably an excellent out-of-the-way meeting place, so who knows? Enjoy it for what it is – an unusual narrow opening in the rocks, where you're some 10 to 15 yards below ground level. You return to the route and soon descend to the River Dane. From here pick your way through the stones and head back to the start.

Refreshments

The **Ship Inn** at Wincle is a marvellous little pub, which dates back to the 1600s. When I visited I really enjoyed their traditional Staffordshire oatcakes filled with cheese and smoked bacon, but there are others items, such as 'Ship Inn' sausages. Telephone: 01260 227217.

THE WALK

Walk down the road away from the **Ship** to cross the **River Dane** by the road bridge. Take the path on the left for '**Gradbach Via Dane Valley**'. After 50 yards climb the concessionary path for '**Hanging Stone**' on your right and 200 yards later ignore a footpath turning sharp right. The path you're on crosses a plank footbridge over a stream. Ascend the path beyond. Climb the stile into the field. Ahead of you is **Hanging Stone**. Walk across the field, keeping to the left of the farm ahead. As you go, keep to the left of a stone in the middle of the field, aiming for the stile beyond. Turn half right uphill beyond the stile. On reaching a track above the farm turn right, passing below **Hanging Stone** itself. Ahead is a view of **The Roaches**, including the rocky outcrop of **Hen Cloud**. On reaching a cattle grid ignore the concessionary path on your left leading uphill to **Hanging Stone** (unless you want to visit it and return to this point).

Keep forward into the open area beyond and bear slightly left to follow the footpath beyond a farmgate. Walk along beside the trees on your right, passing a house shown as '**Paddock**' on the current OS map. Continue walking between a fence on your left and a wall on your right. Pass through another farmgate and bear left up the wide grassy path for Gradbach. This

The view towards Hanging Stone

Lud's Church

soon bears left and becomes a sunken path.

On reaching another gate, with access land beyond, cross the stile and keep forward, still for **Gradbach**, ignoring the path to the right for **Roach End**. Stay on this bridleway for ½ mile until it forks by a rocky outcrop on your left. The walk will continue along the left fork – but feel free to follow the right fork for **Lud's Church** about 250 yards away, and return to this spot.

Lud's Church is a damp, fern-filled chasm, some 30 ft deep and no more than 4 to 5 ft wide at ground level, though it widens out above. It seems to have been named after Walter de Ludauk, a leader of the Lollards, a 14th-century religious group who questioned the role of the Catholic church in England. It may well be that Walter and his followers used to meet at these rocks.

Your route takes you down to the **River Dane**, where you should turn sharp left. Follow the path with the river on your right. Where the path splits, take the right fork beside the river. Stay on the path for a good ½ mile until you leave the woodland by a stile beside a gate. The path you're on rises so that you enter a field. Keep forward to climb a stile and keep on the path between fences. Cross a driveway and continue between fences on the path beyond. There are flocks of different types of sheep in the fields here. Continue on the obvious path, which stays at basically the same height. On reaching a gravel driveway bear right downhill. Pass the property below on your right. Just beyond, walk along a levelish path, dropping slightly perhaps, beside a tumbled-down wall on your left. Enter the woodland again.

Subsequently ignore a grassy track forking left; keep on towards the river. Leave the wood by a stile, following the obvious path with the river to your right. On reaching the road bridge go uphill to your right to return to the **Ship Inn**.

Places of Interest Nearby

Some 4 miles south of Danebridge, on the road to Meerbrook, is **Tittesworth Reservoir**, where you could do a bit of birdwatching, perhaps, or have a stroll round the reservoir itself. Some of the rarities that have been seen here include smews, red kites and little egrets as well as the occasional osprey. There is a small Visitor Centre as well. Telephone: 01538 300400.

10 | Parsley Hay

Cyclists on the High Peak Trail

The Walk 4½ miles
Time 2¼ hours
Map OS Explorer OL24 White Peak GR 147637

How to get there

Parsley Hay is just off the A515 south-west of Monyash. **Parking:** The car park on the High Peak Trail.

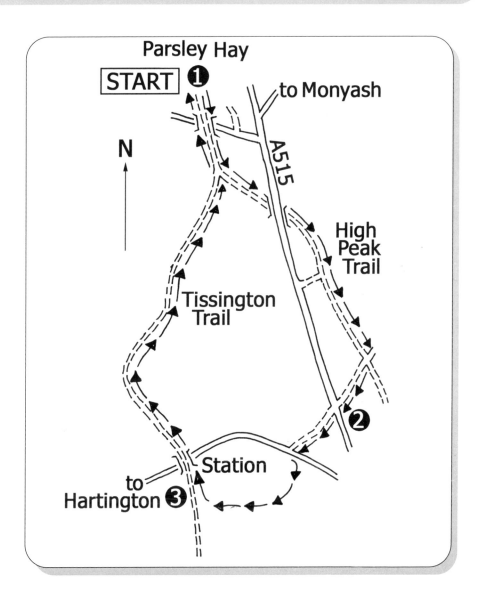

Introduction

This interesting circuit follows firstly the High Peak Trail and then the Tissington Trail, with about a mile of walking on a footpath and a green lane to link the trails. It's generally fairly easy walking without any gradients to

Drive and Stroll

speak of. On a sunny day there's a marvellous clarity in the air. The High Peak Trail follows the route of the former Cromford and High Peak Railway, which ran from Cromford Canal to the Peak Forest Canal, way up in the north of Derbyshire at Whaley Bridge. The Tissington Trail follows the line of what used to be the Ashbourne and Buxton Railway. They both provide an excellent opportunity to walk or ride through the Derbyshire countryside. The stretch from Hartington Station to the High Peak Trail at Parsley Hay forms part of the Pennine Bridleway, and see if you can see any signs of badgers as you head north from the station.

Refreshments

From Parsley Hay drive back to the A515 and turn left. Stay on this for about 2 miles until you reach the **Bull i' th' Thorn** (literally the 'bull in the thorn' and pronounced by us locals as 't' bully thorn') at Hurdlow. It reckons to be at least a 15th-century roadside hostelry and I certainly wouldn't dispute that. The menu offers plenty of choice, ranging from bar snacks to full meals, and on a cold day there's a wonderful open fire. Telephone: 01298 83348.

THE WALK

From the car park walk onto the Trail and turn left. After 500 yards, where it forks, take the narrower **High Peak Trail** to the left. **Friden** is just 2½ miles away, though you won't be going quite that far. Enter a cutting with a bridge ahead (this takes the A515 over the Trail). Pass under the bridge.

As you go under this bridge note the stone plaque referring to Josiah Jessop, the canal engineer who worked for the Cromford and High Peak Railway Company, incorporated in 1825 (or is it 1826?). William Brittlebank also gets a mention – perhaps he was the stonemason.

Pass under another bridge (there are the remains of an old signal just beyond it) before crossing a track, with the A515 about 200 yards to your right. The Trail then passes through the narrow **Blakemoor Plantation** and beyond this the views to your left are longer. Continue for 450 yards after the plantation until you reach another track – **Green Lane** (though it isn't named). Turn right up this for 550 yards to reach the A515.

Cross the road carefully and continue along the track beyond. This descends to a lane leading down to **Hartington** to your right. Turn left, though, for 100 yards. Pass through the wicket gate on your right to enter the **Hartington Meadows Reserve**.

This is the newest of the Derbyshire Wildlife Trust's reserves and is full of colour in summertime. As this is a working farm, the grass is cut in the summer so encouraging the growth of various meadow flowers such as hay rattle.

Proceed along the left side of two fields before bearing slightly right in the third field (still with the wall on your left) to enter a fourth field. Descend this field to pass through a wicket gate. Head across the fifth field, aiming for the right side of a stand of trees. Pass through the wicket gate and continue along the path. This brings you to a stone step-stile. Descend to the **Tissington Trail** beyond.

Turn right to reach **Hartington Station**, with its signal box and toilets.

Hartington Station is the starting point for many local walks and has good parking facilities. It also has a paddock and is the start of the Pennine Bridleway for horseriders. At present the bridleway runs for 120 miles from Derbyshire to the South Pennines. Eventually, it is hoped to create a 347-mile trail.

Proceed northward on the **Tissington Trail.**

Pass through two cuttings and pass **Hartington Moor Farm** down below to your left. Then the Trail crosses a fairly high embankment with the area known as **Parsley Hey** [sic] to your left. There's a 'bird' symbol on the OS map for this area, though there seems to be nothing unusual to see. Pass under a bridge, which brings you to a cutting. Just beyond this the **Tissington Trail** joins the **High Peak Trail**. Keep forward to return to your car.

Places of Interest Nearby

How about heading down to **Hartington**? Being in Derbyshire, Hartington is one of the few places where Stilton cheese can be made and you can buy it in the cheese shop near the duck pond. The youth hostel on the edge of Hartington is housed in Hartington Hall, where Bonnie Prince Charlie is alleged to have stayed on his ill-fated 'invasion' of England in 1745. There are various souvenir shops and a pottery to browse around.

You could then drive *up* the **Dove Valley** by heading north from the centre of Hartington to enjoy a rather different landscape, being wider and lower than that south of the village.

11 Rowthorne

The Rowthorne Trail

The Walk 3¾ miles
Time 2 hours
Map OS Explorer 269 Chesterfield and Alfreton GR 476647

How to get there

Rowthorne lies south of Glapwell, which is on the A617 between the M1 (junction 29) and Pleasley. Just east of the Young Vanish pub in Glapwell, turn off southwards for Rowthorne. **Parking:** Drive through Rowthorne, continuing until you fork left into the car park for the Rowthorne Trail.

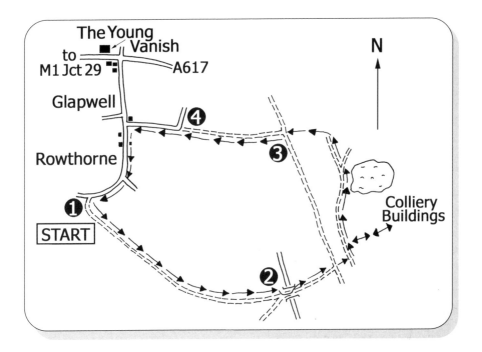

Introduction

This is a gentle walk in a rather lovely part of the world and it will surprise many people. Start off along the Rowthorne Trail, which follows what was originally, of course, an industrial railway line in this once coal-mined area. The route is quite wooded here and if the summer sunshine is percolating through the trees you will be in for a special treat. After 1½ miles you're on the Teversal Trail, for a shorter distance. When I walked it we passed through a flower-rich area brimming with butterflies and other insects. On reaching the Pleasley Colliery Conservation Area, the countryside opens out a bit more and you'll have the chance to view the old colliery. You then make your way back to Rowthorne village, where you may be surprised to learn that some of the farmland around here is owned by the Chatsworth Estate.

this area is proving popular with birdwatchers, too, with over 140 different species of bird having been recorded around here in the last few years, so it's worth having your binoculars with you!

The stony track splits again; take the left fork. As you go you'll see **Hardwick Hall**, half left. The Trail has a packed clay surface, then a grassy one. Ahead, you should be able to see and hear the A617. Swing left between a hedge and fence in the general direction of **Rowthorne**.

 ③

On reaching a track, cross it and take the public footpath (and concessionary bridleway) to **Rowthorne**. Keep forward on this for 600 yards to join the corner of a lane.

 ④

Continue straight ahead on the lane and at the T-junction turn left into the village. At **Hall Farm** ignore the lane to the left – keep straight on and bear right with the lane. Eventually you can bear left, back to the **Rowthorne Trail car park**.

Going through Rowthorne village

12 Alstonefield

Lode Mill

The Walk 3½ miles
Time 2 hours (to allow time to climb the hill into Alstonefield on the way back!)
Map OS Explorer OL24 White Peak GR 131557

How to get there

Alstonefield is 3 miles south of Hartington as the crow flies and reached from the A515 west of Alsop en le Dale or from the B5054 at Hulme End. **Parking:** In the small public car park by the toilets.

Drive and Stroll

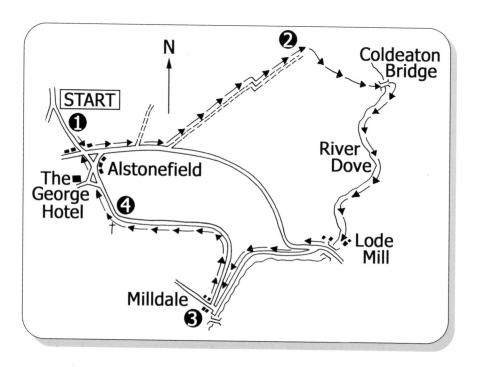

Introduction

The lovely village of Alstonefield and the marvellous scenery of the valley of the River Dove are featured on this short but slightly challenging walk. I've said the circuit will take a couple of hours – it could be longer, because if I were you I would go slowly and savour it. After ½ mile or so, you'll find you're walking along a delightful limestone walled track, with a splendid view down into the dale at the end of it. You descend and then walk downstream, enjoying some gorgeous scenery as you go – and look out for dippers and herons. At Milldale you come to Viator's Bridge and a small National Trust barn, which provides some information about the area. You then have a bit of a slog up the lane back to Alstonefield, with the chance to recover in the churchyard!

Refreshments

The **George Hotel** in Alstonefield is a really popular pub, especially with walkers. It's an old coaching house with lots of atmosphere and good food, including such things as asparagus flan and smoked peppered mackerel fillets. Telephone: 01335 310205.

THE WALK

From the car park turn right up the road. Follow this round to the left. Pass the triangular green on your right. This road is signed for **Lode Mill** and **Ashbourne**. You will soon be leaving **Alstonefield**. Ignore a walled track/footpath on your left for **Narrow Dale** and **Gipsy Bank**. Take the second walled track, which heads for **Coldeaton Bridge** via **Gipsy Bank**. Pass the **Youth Hostel**. Stay on the track, which becomes more rural, for ⅔ mile.

Climb a stile at the end of the track. Bear right, then left into the valley. Cross **Coldeaton Bridge** to reach the Derbyshire side of the **River Dove**. Turn right and follow the path downstream.

Look out for dippers in the river. They are the small brown birds with a white bib that are constantly 'dipping' as they stand on stones in the water.

Dovedale

Drive and Stroll

On reaching the road at **Lode Mill**, cross the bridge and step back into Staffordshire. Turn left along the road for **Milldale**.

Just under ½ mile later you reach **Milldale** with the famous **Viator's Bridge** ahead of you.

There are toilets here and of course Viator's Bridge is forever connected with Izaak Walton who wrote The Compleat Angler *in the 17th century. Walton regularly fished these waters with his good friend Charles Cotton. There's an interesting small National Trust building to the right of the bridge.*

Keep right as you enter **Milldale** to ascend the lane past **Polly's Cottage**. This is signed 'Unsuitable for Motors' but you may get the odd bike passing you. You are climbing **Millway Lane** and it takes you past a **Methodist chapel** (built in 1835). It provides quite a testing climb initially but then levels out. The lane passes **St Peter's church** on your left.

At the main gate leading into the church bear right, back into **Alstonefield** to reach the **George**. Keep forward down the right side of the pub to return to your car.

Places of Interest Nearby

If you enjoy churches look around **St Peter's church** in Alstonefield (if you've got clean shoes). The Cotton family pew is certainly striking, and outside there are a couple of interesting tombstones – one of which dates back to 1518 and the other is in memory of someone who lived to be 107 in the 18th century. Alternatively, drive down to **Ilam** (3 miles south of Alstonefield) and have a short stroll there.

13 | Minninglow

Walking down the green lane into Pikehall

The Walk 3¾ miles
Time Just under 2 hours
Map OS Explorer OL24 White Peak GR 194582

How to get there

From Pikehall on the A5012 between Newhaven and Grangemill, turn south for Parwich. **Parking:** After just over ½ mile turn left for the Minninglow car park.

Drive and Stroll

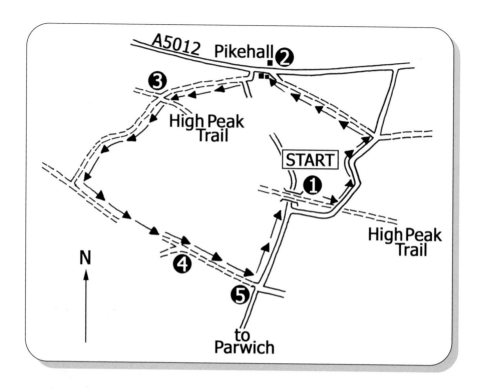

Introduction

A fairly steady and evocative stroll in the White Peak area of the Peak District. To begin with you'll be following a tarmac lane, then a green lane down into Pikehall. Another (newly gravelled) lane takes you out of the village, rising up to and crossing the High Peak Trail with far-reaching views all around. Everywhere you get the feeling that you're in touch with the area's history – the old roads you're using, the former railway line converted to the High Peak Trail. Then you come to that marvellous view of Minninglow over a mile away. This prominent landmark was visited a few thousand years ago by ancient man wanting to make use of such an excellent viewpoint.

Refreshments

From the car park turn right and then left to head south for 2 miles or so. Follow the signs into Parwich and visit the **Sycamore Inn**, next to the church. This is a pub that is very popular with walkers and there's a good choice of food here, with vegetarian dishes such as leek and mushroom crumble and fish dishes such as breaded plaice. Telephone: 01335 390212.

THE WALK

Walk to the lane at the eastern end of the car park as though you were going to cross it to continue along the Trail towards **Cromford**. Don't follow the Trail, though – turn left along the narrow lane.

After a couple of minutes you will see the embankment that carries the Trail on your right. This is just one of the many impressive features on the High Peak Trail. Elsewhere there are very steep inclines such as at Middleton Top, where an engine house was built to allow passage of the engines up and down the incline.

After about 700 yards, on a gentle left-hand bend, a track joins the road from the right; turn left through a gate to follow a track downhill into **Pikehall**.

On reaching the main road turn left along the verge as far as the road for **Parwich**. Follow this as it winds right, then left. On the left-hand bend take the gravel lane leading steadily uphill. As you ascend this, ahead (slightly right), you will see **Aleck Low**, nearly 1,300 ft above sea level.

This lane has recently been resurfaced, as it was becoming badly rutted due to being used by 4x4s. The 4x4 drivers would probably argue the ruts were caused by agricultural vehicles! Suffice to say that the Peak Park authorities are trying to improve the grassy lanes and tracks that run between the Tissington and High Peak Trails – especially for cyclists (though it also benefits walkers).

On reaching the **High Peak Trail** (which is also the **Pennine Bridleway** hereabouts), cross this (unless you want a shorter walk back to the car park, in which case you would turn left along the Trail). Continue along the gravel track, which rises steadily uphill. After ⅔ mile **Cardlemere Lane** joins yours from the right. Turn left and follow the walled track beyond. When the track enters an open field, keep forward on the track, shortly walking beside a wall on your right. The views have opened out by now, with **Minninglow**, the tree-topped hill, being prominent.

Minninglow was the site of a number of burials over 2,000 years ago.

Drive and Stroll

The Sycamore Inn at Parwich

 ④

On reaching another track joining from sharp right, ignore it and head forward towards **Minninglow**.

 ⑤

After ½ mile you reach a tarmac lane (having passed an isolated cottage on your right). Turn left here back to the car park.

Places of Interest Nearby

From the Sycamore Inn at Parwich you could drive east for approximately 4 miles to **Carsington Water**. You can look around the visitor centre or perhaps visit one of the bird hides and do a bit of birdwatching. Telephone: 01629 540696.

14 | Waterhouses

Cyclists on the Manifold Way

The Walk 4½ miles
Time 2½ hours
Map OS Explorer OL24 White Peak GR 085501

How to get there

Waterhouses is on the A523 Leek–Ashbourne road. In the village follow the signs for 'Manifold Track Cycle Hire Centre' to the south of the main road to reach the start of this walk. **Parking:** In the car park of the Cycle Hire Centre.

Drive and Stroll

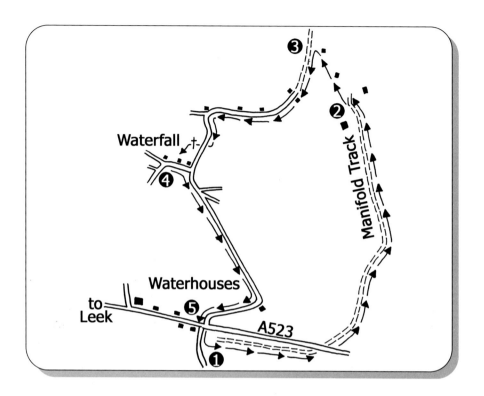

Introduction

A gentle walk right at the southern end of the Peak District – and not all that busy. From Waterhouses the Manifold Track leads you northwards, providing a level start to the route. After a good mile you leave it behind to climb diagonally across the fields to a splendid vantage point above the valley. Stop and savour the view from here. Then a very quiet narrow lane brings you into Back o' th' Brook and subsequently to the church of St James and St Bartholomew, which stands alone and is often referred to informally as the 'church in a field'. Continue into Waterfall and you'll start to guess there's something of a theme developing, what with Back o' th' Brook, Waterfall and Waterhouses . . . Then Rocester Lane, which is another quiet lane, takes you back to the start.

Refreshments

The **George Inn**, Leek Road, Waterhouses, offers 'good food; real ale; great atmosphere' – and I wouldn't disagree. Fish is very popular here; so look out for dishes like spicy prawns or Thai-style home-made salmon and crab fishcakes. When you get back to the A523 from the car park turn left and you will reach the George on your right, ¼ mile away. Telephone: 01538 308804.

THE WALK

①

From the car park walk along the **Manifold Track** away from the entrance. Look out for cyclists as you go, and remember you're sharing the track with them.

The track slopes down to the main road. Turn right along the road. As it starts to rise, cross to the left-hand side, go over a bridge and follow the **Manifold Track** again. To your left is **Brownend Cycle Hire**. The tarmac 'track' is easy to follow and you will soon leave behind the noise of the A523. The **River Hamps** should be on your right for quite a way (assuming there's water in it), but you then cross it so it's on your left. Go over the river again so it's back on your right. Just beyond this bridge the track bends gently round to the left, and there's a farm at the top of the field on your left. A small stone bridge takes you over a stream 10 yards later; on your left, pass through a kissing gate.

②

With your back to the kissing gate, turn right to pass through a farmgate. Follow the grassy track beyond into the wood. Once you're back in the open, keep to the left of the stone building to walk into the far left corner.

Pass through a small gate and swing right to cross a stile after 15 yards. Go through a second gate, then a third. Head towards the left side of a stone building to reach another 'bridlegate' beyond it. Keep forward along the line of trees to reach a small lane.

③

Turn left here. There are good views across the valley. Keep on the track, passing straight through the property of **Redwayclose Barn** and descend beyond, continuing for ½ mile. At **Brockhouse Farm** in **Back o' th' Brook**, the lane swings left downhill. Bear left, almost immediately, off the lane you're on, onto another, crossing a ford as you go. The lane then rises quite steeply, and, 400 yards after joining it, just beyond a cottage, take the track to the **church of St James and St Bartholomew**.

Inside there's a splendid (crooked) chancel arch, which is Norman or earlier.

Assuming you walk down the left-hand side of the church to the porch, on reaching it bear half left down the concrete path to a stile. Turn left beyond this, alongside the hedge on your left, to reach a house on your right. Walk along the grass and the driveway beyond to reach the green in **Waterfall** with its well and stocks.

Drive and Stroll

The seat near the start of the walk from Waterhouses

④

Turn left along the road, passing a cottage on the corner. After 150 yards ignore the lane to the church and bear right. You reach a pinfold on your left after 60 yards. Keep forward, ignoring a couple of lanes to the left (both signed 'No Through Road'). Stay on this road (it's **Rocester Lane**, though it may not be signed as such) for ¾ mile until it turns sharp right. Keep on it to reach the main road.

⑤

Turn right for a few yards and cross the road to head back to the start. Immediately beyond **Station House** fork left to reach the car park.

Places of Interest Nearby

Why not travel further up the Manifold Track by bike and see where else you can explore on foot another day? Contact the **Cycle Hire Centre** (telephone: 01538 308609). Alternatively, get in your car and go and explore **Grindon**, **Wetton**, **Butterton** and **Ilam**. These are all quiet, attractive Staffordshire villages – higgledy-piggledy in nature and all within 5 or 6 miles of Waterhouses. Look out for the ford at the southern end of Butterton – and the ducks that paddle in it!

15 | **Black Rocks, Cromford**

The view from the High Peak Trail

The Walk 3½ miles
Time 2 hours
Map OS Explorer OL24 White Peak GR 291557

How to get there

Black Rocks lies to the east of the B5036 between Cromford and Wirksworth. Approaching from Cromford, when you near the top of Cromford Hill fork left to reach the Black Rocks car park. **Parking:** Take the second entrance on the left to park beyond the toilet block.

Drive and Stroll

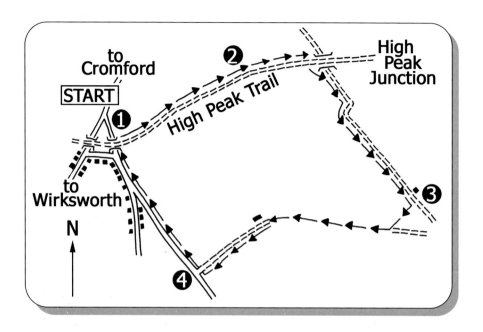

Introduction

Marvellous views abound as you enjoy this walk. You're straight onto the High Peak Trail at the beginning and the level start gives glorious views across the Derwent Valley as you survey Cromford, High Tor and, beyond that, Matlock. You should be able to spot Willersley Castle and the redbrick Masson Mill. A little further along you pass a pond where you may see some newts at the right time of year. Then beyond that you reach the top of Sheep Pasture Incline. Just imagine a steam train going up or down here – even cyclists are advised to dismount. But wouldn't it have been a majestic site? Part of the way down the Incline, the walk leaves the Trail and you follow Intake Lane for a mile or so before rising up through the fields to come out above Wirksworth The final stretch of the walk is along the road through Bolehill. Just uphill from the car park is the rocky outcrop known as Black Rocks or, sometimes, just Black Rock. Locals tend to call it Black Rocks. It's popular with climbers and with people who are prepared to scramble up to the top (it's not *too* difficult) to enjoy the striking views across the Derwent Valley – a view you'll be able to enjoy on the walk with less of a threat to life and limb!

Refreshments

The delightful **Malt Shovel Inn** on Oakerthorpe Road, Wirksworth Moor, is ½ mile south of point 4. It's unusual (and all the better for it) because it's an easy-going country pub, open to all. Walkers can even take their *own* sandwiches as long as they buy a drink each. Between 12 noon and 2 pm though you can get a sandwich (toasted or otherwise) with some chips thrown in if you wish. There's not a wide range of food but that's not what the Malt Shovel is all about. Telephone: 01629 822427.

THE WALK

Turn left along the **High Peak Trail**. Follow this, passing through the LNWR boundary posts. Stay on the Trail as it passes beneath the trees, intermittently coming out in the open to give fine views across **Cromford**, **Willersley Castle** and **Masson Mill's redbrick chimney**, with **High Tor** beyond that and **Matlock** in the background.

You reach **Sheep Pasture Top** (with the remains of the **engine house**, opened in May 1830).

The engine here used to haul wagons up the 1 in 8 incline you will be walking down. There's a catchpit right at the bottom of the incline (which you won't see on this walk) and this has recently been renovated.

Keep forward to descend the incline. After 500 yards fork right on the path signed for **Alderwasley** and the **Midshires Way**.

The Midshires Way is 225 miles long and links the Ridgeway with the Trans Pennine Trail at Stockport. There's an excellent guidebook written by Ron Haydock and Bill Allen, and Ron only lives about a mile from this spot!

Ignore a path to the right (rising up steps) shortly after. On reaching a track, bear right, ignoring the turn to the left, which takes the track under the incline. This track is actually **Intake Lane**. Walk beside a wall on your right with a drop to your left, and after 300 yards follow the track round to the right, ignoring a path heading forward. Less than 100 yards later the track bears left and the scenery changes as you walk along a walled track between walls. Stay on Intake Lane for ½ mile to reach a path crossing the lane (immediately beyond a corrugated sheet barn on your left).

Take the stile on your right and walk up the left side of the first three fields. In the fourth field keep forward across the top to pass through a squeezer stile, ignoring a step-stile to its left.

Drive and Stroll

An unusual seat on the High Peak Trail – carved with a chainsaw!

This brings you to a gate at the top of a track on your left. In this fifth field bear half right up the grassy track to the gate at the top. Stay on the track to reach a bridlegate at the top of field six. Proceed up the left side of the next field to pass through a farmgate and walk up the bridleway as it runs through the gorse bushes. This brings you to a farmtrack, which you should bear left along to reach another gate.

Follow the track for ½ mile to the road, passing **Wigwellnook Farm** as you go. (The **Malt Shovel Inn** is ½ mile away to your left.)

Turn right along the road for just over ½ mile. Where it bends left, turn right under the bridge and subsequently right again when you reach the car park entrance to get back to your car.

Places of Interest Nearby

Wirksworth, at one time an ancient leadmining village, is well worth exploring, and there are quite a few attractions in the area. You could visit the **Ecclesbourne Valley Railway** (telephone: 01629 823076), the **National Stone Centre** (telephone: 01629 824833) and **Steeple Grange Light Railway** (telephone: 01246 205542) – so much to do – so little time to do it in.

16 Osmaston

One of the ponds on the Osmaston walk

The Walk 3½ miles
Time 1¾ hours
Map OS Explorer 259 Derby GR 199439

How to get there

Turn off the A52 on the southern edge of Ashbourne for Osmaston.
Parking: Use the village hall car park, on the right as you enter the
village. The Shoulder of Mutton is just a little further along, on the left.

Drive and Stroll

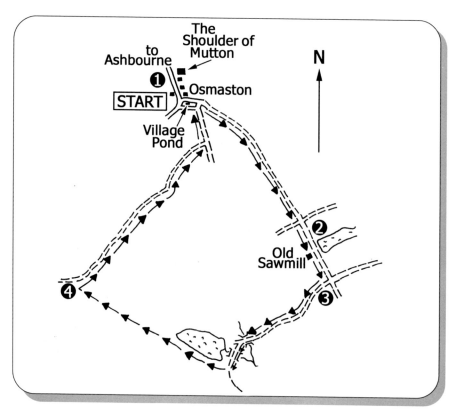

Introduction

I don't know how many times I've encouraged people to visit Osmaston but it seems like a lot. I'll keep singing its praises though because I can't imagine you would be disappointed walking around here. With its picture postcard thatched cottages you're off to a good start. Pass the village pond and you'll be heading along the Bonnie Prince Charlie Walk for Shirley. The prince would have gone in this general direction when he came down from Scotland in 1745. Okay he probably wouldn't have gone exactly along this route but who knows, he was somewhere nearby. A track heading downhill brings you to Osmaston Sawmill, one of the most photographed of Derbyshire buildings I should think and one that has featured on TV occasionally. There is then a short sharp climb, which will get your heart a-pounding before you descend a track under the trees to reach the valley. A lovely large pond is then on your right and you walk to the far end of this before continuing up the valley to pick up the track that leads you back to the start.

Refreshments

The **Shoulder of Mutton** in Osmaston is also a post office – a novel idea but also a good one – so you can get stamps here as well as food and drink. There's a wide choice of things to eat, ranging from 'jackets' to toasties to sandwiches to specials (such as beef and walnut casserole or lamb, apricot and mushroom pie). Telephone: 01335 342371.

THE WALK

 ①

With your back to the **Shoulder of Mutton**, turn left along the road, passing attractive brick houses, some of them thatched. At the village pond turn left on the road between a thatched cottage on your left and the pond itself. With a number of options open to you, keep forward along the bridleway for **Shirley** – a level gravel track passing between gateposts. You're also following the **Bonnie Prince Charlie Walk**.

The Bonnie Prince Charlie Walk was devised in 1995 by members of the Ramblers' Association to mark the 60th anniversary of their formation. It follows the general line of the Prince's march into Derby, though he didn't get much further than that, of course, being forced to turn back as his army deserted him.

The bridleway crosses an open field before you enter a wood. Continue through this and proceed beyond. Ignore a private track to the left, as you keep forward to enter a second wood. Beyond this descend to a crossroads of tracks. Continue

forward towards the valley bottom and the delightful sawmill ahead.

 ②

There is usually plenty of wildfowl on the pond to your left.

I have seen Canada, pink-footed and barnacle geese here.

With the sawmill to your right, follow the steep gravel track uphill underneath the trees. A fairly testing 250 yards later the ground levels out. You reach a crossroads of tracks. Turn right here.

 ③

Follow the track downhill, ignoring all tracks to left and right. After ½ mile you reach a brook. Cross this and fork left a few yards later. Go over another brook and proceed to the farmgate ahead. Turn right beyond. Walk beside a pond on your right. On reaching a fenced area, cross the stile and proceed to the far end. In the fields beyond proceed for less than ½ mile in the valley bottom.

 ④

You reach a track heading sharp right into a wood. Follow this through the gate. Stay on this for some way to

Osmaston village and pond

reach a brick and black and white timbered property on your left. Pass it and proceed along the tarmac drive ahead, forking left 50 yards later.

Osmaston Hall was demolished in the 1960s and all that remains is a tower, which you may have glimpsed earlier in the walk.

Ignore a track to the left and then one to the right to reach the sports field known as the **Polo Ground** on your left. Bear slightly right here before turning left on joining an access road. Walk towards **Osmaston church** ahead of you to reach the village, where you can return to your car.

Places of Interest Nearby

There are a couple of options. Drive along the A52 into **Ashbourne** and have a walk round – try and visit **St Oswald's church**. The alternative is to head south-east for 5 miles and visit 18th-century **Kedleston Hall**. This is another National Trust property well worth exploring. Telephone: 01332 842191.

17 | Farnah Green

A view from North Lane near Farnah Green

The Walk 4½ miles
Time 2¼ hours
Map OS Explorer 259 Derby GR 335463

How to get there

Farnah Green lies to the south of the A517 Belper–Ashourne road. Less than a mile from Belper turn off southwards at the crossroads for Hazelwood. **Parking:** Proceed for just over a mile until you reach a lay-by on the left, where you can park your car.

Drive and Stroll

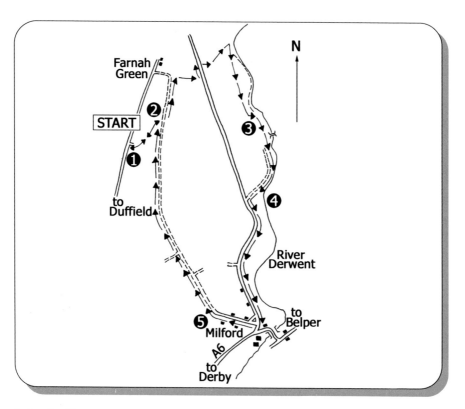

Introduction

We all drive along the A6 and fail, perhaps, to be aware of the 'stonking' views there are nearby – what you will see on this walk may well surprise you. To start with, you follow North Lane, an ancient byway running along a ridge above the valley. The trees provide a frame here and there for the views of Belper below. A path then leads you down into the Derwent Valley, where you turn south alongside the river until a lane takes you into Milford with its old millworkers' cottages. There is then a steep climb straight up Sunny Hill, but take your time, enjoy the views behind you and the houses all around you . . . and before you know it you'll be at the summit. From there you're back onto North Lane, which is quite wide in parts under the trees. It's also popular with walkers wanting to escape the hustle and bustle of modern life just a few hundred yards away. Enjoy.

Refreshments

The **Mill House** in Milford is a new pub and part of the Mill House group. It is nicely positioned right beside the Derwent, so on fine days you can sit at one of the tables outside and watch the river flow past. The menu offers plenty of choice – three bean chilli, Thai red chicken curry or minted lamb shoulder, for example. To reach the pub from the lay-by south of Farnah Green, proceed along the road for Duffield. At the first junction turn left. Stay on this road to reach the A6 nearly 2 miles later. Then turn left along the A6 to turn right for the Mill House as you enter Milford. Telephone: 01332 843144.

THE WALK

From your car walk north, turning right on the path at the end of the lay-by. Keep left on this path until 450 yards after joining it you reach a stony lane. Remember this – it's the way back!

Turn left for 300 yards along this lane (**North Lane**, though it's not signed as such) with a marvellous view of **Belper** to your right. Just before the left turn take the path on your right. Walk down the left side of two fields to the lane. Turn left for 120 yards, then right along the driveway. At the far end, cross the stile and bear left diagonally downhill. A paved stretch of path leads you into a second field. Continue in this direction in a third field then a fourth. When the path levels out turn right towards the stile by a gate. Beyond this the official path heads straight forward for nearly 500 yards. However, everybody seems to walk on the left beside the river. In the next field, again people stay by the river though according to the map they should keep straight ahead.

Keep between the river on your left and the sewage works fence on your right. Pass under a footbridge. On reaching an access road bear left to reach a T-junction.

Turn left. Stay on this road for about a mile, crossing the railway line with an impressive tunnel entrance to your right. Pass the old mill cottages as you proceed.

It always interests me that delightful cottages like these are so popular nowadays. I am sure that the underpaid and overworked millworkers who used to live here would be absolutely flabbergasted if they could see how much better off people are nowadays – and that's how it should be of course.

On reaching **Milford Primary School** turn right up **Sunny Hill**. It has to be said there's a steep climb for nearly 400 yards. There are interesting houses as you go though. At the top of the hill there is a trig point to your right. Follow the main track forward then bear right, away from the desirable residences thereabouts.

Drive and Stroll

A train heads into the tunnel

The walk changes character very quickly, and you'll see an unusual tower behind the cottage on your right.

This appears to have been a sighting tower, connected presumably with the construction of the railway tunnel, which passes underground nearby.

This old track you're now on passes through **Chevin golf course**. Ignore a track to your left hereabouts. Subsequently ignore a track downhill to your right, and then a path to your left

on the **Derwent Valley Heritage Way**.

The Derwent Valley Heritage Way is a 55-mile-long walk from Heatherdene car park near Ladybower to Derwent Mouth near Shardlow. It follows (as you may have guessed) the route of the River Derwent – and there's a guidebook that describes it.

You then pass a 30 ft high wall standing at an angle to the track – an old shooting area perhaps? After 600 yards turn sharp left up the path you used earlier. As you return along this path, keep right to get back to the lay-by.

Places of Interest Nearby

Belper is an interesting mill town and worth exploring. A walk around the **Riverside Gardens** is a nice way of unwinding, too. You could travel a few miles north and visit **Crich Tramway Village** – home to the National Tramway Museum. Telephone: 01773 854321.

18 | Mickleover

Walkers head across the fields towards Radbourne

The Walk 4¼ miles
Time 2 hours
Map OS Explorer 259 Derby GR 309360

How to get there

Mickleover lies south of the A52 between Derby and Ashbourne. Approaching from Derby, follow the A52 north-west and pass the crematorium sign to the right. Subsequently turn left for Radbourne. A mile later turn left into Station Road. The Great Northern pub is 450 yards later on the left. **Parking:** In the pub car park if you are a customer, or on-street nearby.

Drive and Stroll

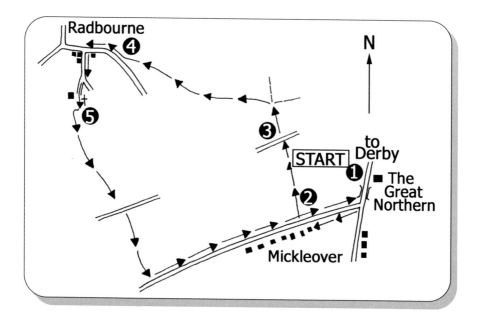

Introduction

On the western side of Derby, paths between Mickleover and Radbourne provide a rather lovely, gentle, stroll that will surprise many people, especially those from outside Derby itself. The recent opening of Cycleway 54, the Mickleover Trail, from Mickleover to Egginton, has provided about a third of this route and is full of interest as birds fly around in the trees beside the old railway line. So, the walk starts and finishes on the Cycleway but in between there is some leisurely and interesting strolling to be done across the fields to the lovely hamlet of Radbourne. The proof is in the pudding, of course, so get out there and enjoy this delightful, somewhat understated area.

Refreshments

The **Great Northern** in Mickleover has modern decor inside and a nice atmosphere. The food is very good and I can recommend the various options, which are described as 'Little Dishes', 'Melts', 'Meatless Dishes', 'Combos' and 'Leaves', ranging from chicken Caesar salad to topped foccacia bread. Telephone: 01332 514288.

THE WALK

NB: There may be a bit of mud here and there in the fields, so be prepared.

Turn left on the road from the **Great Northern**. Cross the old bridge. Immediately beyond, turn right into the open area ahead and follow the Trail (signed '**Burton**' and '**Ashbourne**'). You will now be on Cycleway routes 54 and 68.

The Sustrans website states that it is 'the UK's leading sustainable transport charity, working on practical projects so people can choose to travel in ways that benefit their health and the environment'. I have no connection with the charity but I admire what it is trying to achieve, and this cycleway is part of it. Keep up the good work!

Keep forward to reach a number of houses, presumably the old station buildings, on your right. Pass through the barriers and proceed along the left side of the area ahead and continue on the Trail beyond.

After ⅓ mile you reach a flight of wooden steps on your right. Climb these. Walk forward along the left side of three fields to reach a lane.

Cross the lane to climb the stile to the right of the farmgate. Walk down the right side of the first field to reach a footbridge in the corner. Don't cross this – turn left in this first field and walk parallel to a hedge on your right towards a hedge corner sticking out in the field ahead. Climb the stile in the small

Radbourne church

A milepost on National Cycleway 54 at Mickleover

section of fencing in the hedge. In the field beyond, the path should actually be some way from the hedge on your left, but most people seem to walk down the left side of the field, beside the hedge. On reaching the electricity lines ahead, turn right underneath them. Follow the lines through the rest of this second field and then a third one. With redbrick farm buildings to your left, pass through a gap and cross the corner of the fourth field, aiming for a half dead oak tree. Keep in the same direction beyond this tree to reach the far bottom corner of the fifth field.

Turn right along the lane and follow it all the way into **Radbourne**. Turn left immediately past the pair of semi-detached houses on your left to walk along **School Lane** towards the **parish church of St Andrew**. Keep forward until the lane splits, taking the right fork. Pass **School House** on your right. Enter the churchyard beyond.

Inside the church you will find monuments to the de la Pole family, whose ancestors built nearby Radbourne Hall.

At the end of the church, with the porch on your left, turn right to the kissing gate. Pass through this and turn left through a pair of farmgates at both ends of a bridge. Follow the grassy track beyond for 200 yards. With the corner of a wood on your right, bear *slightly* left off the track, aiming for the left side of a wood another 200 yards ahead. Walk down the left side of this wood to reach the bottom of the field. Pass through the small gate here into the wood and follow the path to the lane.

Cross the lane and pass through a small gate, climbing the stile beyond. Keep straight forward through the first field, then the second. In the third bear slightly left, away from the hedge on your right, to reach a stile. Keep in the same direction in the fourth field to reach a stile to enter **Black Wood**. Cross the footbridge and keep forward for 20 yards to reach the Trail.

Turn left for a mile along the Trail back to the start.

Places of Interest Nearby

Some 10 miles south-west of Mickleover, and reached from the A50, is **Sudbury Hall**, which is well worth visiting. This National Trust property was featured in the BBC's *Pride and Prejudice,* so you might recognise the odd nook or cranny. Telephone: 01332 583337. Alternatively head into **Derby** itself – there's plenty to do, including visiting **Derby Museum and Art Gallery**. Telephone: 01332 716659.

19 | Weston on Trent

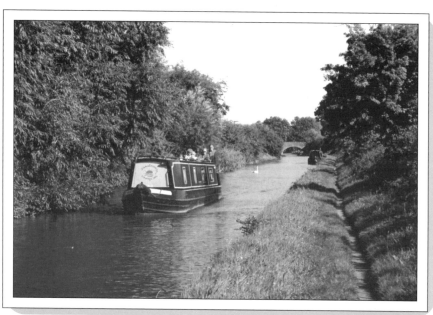

A narrowboat on the Trent and Mersey Canal

The Walk 2¼ miles
Time 1¼ hours
Map OS Explorer 245 The National Forest GR 404280

How to get there

Weston on Trent is south-east of Derby. Assuming you're on the A50, take the road for Melbourne at the large roundabout on the edge of Chellaston. Just before the canal, turn left for Weston. **Parking:** In Trent Lane, or on the main road near the village hall.

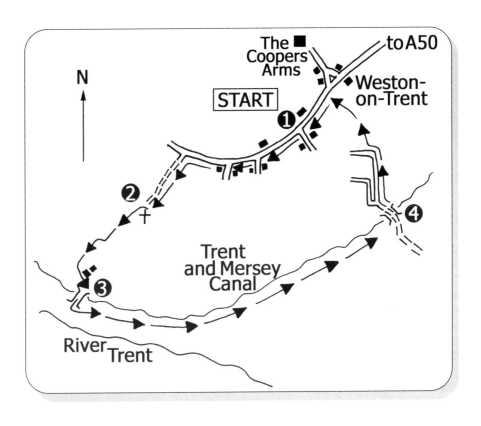

Introduction

A short, gentle stroll in a very interesting area. Well worth visiting, especially if you like canals and exploring somewhere new. The village has some attractive old properties, in particular the Coopers Arms, which used to be Weston Hall. After you've got as far as the church you might fancy sitting down and relaxing in the churchyard with the gravestones lined up against the wall. You're then about twenty minutes from the Trent and Mersey Canal, and, you know canals, there's always something happening on them. Whether it's the fishermen with their long fibreglass rods, the narrowboats cruising by or the wildlife, I can guarantee that there'll be something to watch. Enjoy this stretch of waterside strolling, as it really is lovely. You cross a few fields to return to Weston, walking up the side of the Plough as you go. When you get back to the road, ahead of you there's a grass triangle – the Coopers Arms is up that road – so you'll know where to go once you've got back to the car.

20 Draycott

St Chad's Water at Church Wilne

The Walk 3 miles
Time 1½ hours
Map OS Explorer 260 Nottingham GR 443331

How to get there

Draycott is on the A6005 between Long Eaton and Derby. Approaching from the west, take the turning on the right (Market Street) for Church Wilne and the parish church. **Parking:** In the vicinity of the Methodist chapel built in 1865 and the Methodist church built in 1897, on the right as you drive along Market Street.

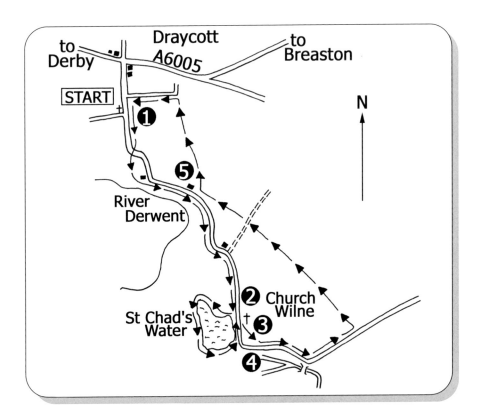

Introduction

No hills on this walk – and don't forget to take your binoculars with you. It's a fascinating route and very different from the hills and dales of the Peak District – but none the worse for that. If you like walking, then you'll enjoy this circuit! The stretch beside the River Derwent is delightful. At Church Wilne do walk round St Chad's Water and have a look in the churchyard too. The inward route follows the Midshires Way, and before you know it you're back at Draycott. But don't rush this walk – just because it says the route will take 1½ hours doesn't mean to say you have to stick to it.

Drive and Stroll

Refreshments

The **Bulls Head**, on the main road in Breaston is a nice pub with a varied menu, which includes Old English fish pie and sweet and sour chicken, followed by hot puddings such as apple and blackberry crumble. From Draycott, return to the A6005 and turn right for approximately 2 miles to reach Breaston. Look out on the left for the Bulls Head. Telephone: 01332 872118.

THE WALK

Head south along the single track lane (with passing places). As the road does a left turn, keep forward along the path between hedges. Come out into the open and beyond the embankment is the **River Derwent**. Walk along this to the left to pass a building on the left side of the road after 200 yards. Stay on the embankment, passing through a kissing gate. Ignore a riverside path hereabouts; stay on the banking beside the road. When the lane takes a gentle left-hand turn, come off the path by a gate (with a **Derbyshire Angling Club** notice on it). Proceed along the lane until you reach a church.

If you are here in September you should see great numbers of hops in the hedges. This suggests that in the past hops have been grown in the area for beer making.

With the church on your left, turn right into the car park and walk all the way around **St Chad's Water**. I will leave you to choose which direction you go. It's usually worth it for the wildlife.

When I was last here, there had been sightings of a white cheeked pintail and an Australian black swan. It's not just the wildfowl you should be looking out for, though. There seemed to be lots of butterflies around when we walked here in summer.

When you get back have a walk around the churchyard.

Our route takes us past the church. At the end of the wood on the left (just beyond the churchyard) pass through a gap and follow the path beside the hedge on your left. Climb a stile and keep in the same direction in the second field.

Turn left on the single track lane. Pass a footbridge over the **Derwent** on your right. After ¼ mile turn left on a bridleway (with a footpath running parallel to it over the other side of the ditch). Follow whichever one you prefer. Walk straight forward for ½ mile to reach another bridleway. Turn

The river Derwent near Draycott

right for 5 or 6 yards before turning left over a stile and following the **Midshires Way**. You may have realised you have been following this since the footbridge over the Derwent.

The Midshires Way links the Ridgeway with the Trans Pennine Trail 225 miles away. Haydock and Allen's Walking the Midshires Way is the guidebook you'll need if you're wanting to tackle this long walk.

Walk along the embankment ahead. Cross a number of stiles as you go to reach the lane you used earlier.

 ⑤

Bear right along this to turn right on a path beside a tall metal fence. Keep forward across a field, following the **Midshires Way** back into **Draycott**. With **Draycott Lodge** on your right, turn left along the road until, with the **Rose and Crown** in front of you, you can turn left back to your car.

Places of Interest Nearby

Keep on beyond Breaston along the A6005 until 3 miles or so later you reach **Attenborough Nature Centre**. Here there are plenty of things to see – birds, a visitor centre, ponds, – and you could wind up the day by having a snack in the Reflections Café. Telephone: 01159 721777.